The Doll And Her Friends: Or Memoirs Of The Lady Seraphina

Mrs. Fairstar

THE
Doll and Her Friends;

OR,

Memoirs of the Lady Seraphina.

EDITED BY

MRS. FAIRSTAR.

With Illustrations by Frank M. Gregory.

New York:
BRENTANO'S

PARIS   WASHINGTON   CHICAGO   LONDON

PREFACE.

MY principal intention, or rather aim, in writing this little book, was to amuse Children by a story founded on one of their favorite diversions, and to inculcate a few such minor morals as my little plot might be strong enough to carry; chiefly the domestic happiness produced by kind tempers and consideration for others. And further, I wished to say a word in favor of that good old-fashioned plaything, the Doll, which one now sometimes hears decried by sensible people who have no children of their own

THE DOLL AND HER FRIENDS.

CHAPTER I.

I BELONG to a race, the sole end of whose existence is to give pleasure to others. None will deny the goodness of such an end, and I flatter myself most persons will allow that we amply fulfil it. Few of the female sex especially but will acknowledge, with either the smile or the sigh called forth by early recollections, that much of their youthful happiness was due to our presence; and some will even go so far as to attribute to our influence many a habit of housewifery, neatness, and industry, which ornaments their riper years.

But to our *influence*, our silent, unconscious influence alone, can such advantages be ascribed; for neither example nor precept are in our power; our race

cannot boast of intellectual endowments;
and though there are few qualities, moral
or mental, that have not in their turn been
imputed to us by partial friends, truth
obliges me to confess that they exist
rather in the minds of our admirers than
in our own persons.

We are a race of mere dependents; some
might even call us slaves.   Unable to
change our place, or move hand or foot
at our own pleasure, and forced to submit
to every caprice of our possessors, we cannot be said to have even a will of our own.
But every condition has its share of good
and evil, and I have often considered my
helplessness and dependence as mere trifles
compared with the troubles to which poor
sensitive human beings are subject.

Pain, sickness, or fatigue I never knew.
While a fidgety child cannot keep still for
two minutes at a time, I sit contentedly
for days together in the same attitude;
and I have before now seen one of those
irritable young mortals cry at a scratch,
while I was bearing needles drawn in and
out of every part of my body, or sitting
with a pin run straight through my heart,

calmly congratulating myself on being free from the inconveniences of flesh and blood.

Of negative merits I possess a good share. I am never out of humor, never impatient, never mischievous, noisy nor intrusive; and though I and my fellows cannot lay claim to brilliant powers either in word or deed, we may boast of the same qualifications as our wittiest king, for certainly none of us ever "said a foolish thing," if she "never did a wise one."

Personal beauty I might almost, without vanity, call the "badge of all our tribe." Our very name is seldom mentioned without the epithet *pretty;* and in my own individual case I may say that I have always been considered pleasing and elegant, though others have surpassed me in size and grandeur.

But our most striking characteristic is our power of inspiring strong attachment. The love bestowed on us by our possessors is proof against time, familiarity, and misfortune:

> "Age cannot wither us, nor custom stale
> Our infinite variety."

With no trace of our original beauty left,
—dress in tatters, complexion defaced,
features undistinguishable, our very limbs
mutilated, the mere wreck of our former
selves,—who has not seen one of us still the
delight and solace of some tender young
heart; the confidant of its fancies, and
the soother of its sorrows; preferred to all
newer claimants, however high their pretensions; the still unrivalled favorite, in
spite of the laughter of the nursery and
the quiet contempt of the school-room?

Young and gentle reader, your sympathy or your sagacity has doubtless suggested to you my name. I am, as you
guess, a Doll; and though not a doll of
any peculiar pretensions, I flatter myself
that my life may not be quite without interest to the young lovers of my race, and
in this hope I venture to submit my memoirs to your indulgent consideration.

I am but a small doll; not one of those
splendid specimens of wax modelled from
the Princess Royal, with distinct fingers
and toes, eyes that shut, and tongues that
wag. No; such I have only contemplated
from a respectful distance as I lay on my

stall in the bazaar, while they towered sub-
lime in the midst of the toys, the wonder
and admiration of every passing child.   I
am not even one of those less magnificent,
but still dignified, leathern-skinned indi-
viduals, requiring clothes to take off and
put on, and a cradle to sleep in, with
sheets, blankets, and everything complete.   Neither can I found my claim to
notice upon anything odd or unusual in
my appearance: I am not a negro doll,
with wide mouth and woolly hair; nor a
doll with a gutta-percha face, which can
be twisted into all kinds of grimaces.

I am a simple English doll, about six
inches high, with jointed limbs and an en-
amel face, a slim waist and upright figure,
an amiable smile, an intelligent eye, and
hair dressed in the first style of fashion.   I
never thought myself vain, but I own that
in my youth I did pique myself upon my
hair.   There was but one opinion about
that.   I have often heard even grown-up
people remark, "How ingeniously that
doll's wig is put on, and how nicely it is
arranged!" while at the same time my ris-
ing vanity was crushed by the insinuation

that I had an absurd smile or a ridiculous stare.

However, the opinions of human beings of mature age never much disturbed me. The world was large enough for them and me; and I could contentedly see them turn to their own objects of interest, while I awaited in calm security the unqualified praise of those whose praise alone was valuable to me—their children and grandchildren.

I first opened my eyes to the light in the Pantheon Bazaar. How I came there I know not; my conscious existence dates only from the moment in which a silver paper covering was removed from my face, and the world burst upon my view. A feeling of importance was the first that arose in my mind. As the hand that held me turned me from side to side, I looked about. Dolls were before me, dolls behind, and dolls on each side. For a considerable time I could see nothing else. The world seemed made for dolls. But by degrees, as my powers of vision strengthened, my horizon extended, and I perceived that portions of space were allotted to many other objects. I descried, at various distances, aids to amusements in endless succession,—balls, bats, battledores, boxes, bags, and baskets, carts, cradles, and cups and saucers. I did not then know anything of the alphabet, and I cannot say that I have quite mastered it even now; but if I were learned enough, I am sure I could go from A to Z, as initial letters of the wonders with which I soon made acquaintance.

Not that I at once became aware of the uses, or even the names, of all I saw. No one took the trouble to teach me; and it was only by dint of my own intense observation that I gained any knowledge at all. I did not at first even know that I was a doll. But I made the most of opportunities, and my mind gradually expanded.

I first learned to distinguish human beings. Their powers of motion made a decided difference between them and the other surrounding objects, and naturally my attention was early turned toward the actions of the shopwoman on whose stall I lived. She covered me and my companions with a large cloth every night, and restored the daylight to us in the morning. We were all perfectly helpless without her, and absolutely under her control. At her will the largest top hummed, or was silent; the whip cracked, or lay harmlessly by the side of the horse. She moved us from place to place, and exhibited or hid us at her pleasure; but she was always so extremely careful of our health and looks, and her life seemed so entirely devoted to us and to our advantage, that I often doubted whether she was our property or we hers. Her habits varied so little from day to day, that after watching her for a reasonable time, I felt myself perfectly acquainted with *her*, and in a condition to make observations upon others of her race.

One day a lady and a little girl stopped at our stall.

"Oh, what a splendid doll!" exclaimed the child, pointing to the waxen beauty which outshone the rest of our tribe. It was the first time I had heard the word *Doll*, though I was well acquainted with the illustrious individual to whom it was applied; and it now flashed upon my mind, with pride and pleasure, that, however insignificant in comparison, I too was a doll. But I had not time to think very deeply about my name and nature just then, as I wished to listen to the conversation of the two human beings.

"May I buy her?" said the little girl.

"Can you afford it?" asked the lady in return. "Remember your intentions for your brother."

"Perhaps I have money enough for both," answered the child. "How much does she cost?"

"Seven shillings," said the shopwoman, taking the doll from her place and displaying her pretty face and hands to the utmost advantage.

"I have three half crowns," said the little girl.

"But if you spend seven shillings on the doll," answered the lady, "you will only have sixpence left for the paint-box."

"What does a paint-box cost?" asked the child.

"We have them of all prices," replied the shopkeeper; "from sixpence to seven shillings."

The little girl examined several with great care, and stood some time in deliberation; at last she said, "I don't think Willy would like a sixpenny one."

"It would be of no use to him," answered the lady. "He draws well enough to want better colors. If you gave it to him, he would thank you and try to seem pleased, but he would not really care for it. However, he does not know that you thought of making him a birthday present, so you are at liberty to spend your money as you like."

"Would he care for a seven-shilling one?" asked the little girl.

"Yes; that is exactly what he wants."

"Then he shall have it," exclaimed the good-natured little sister. "Poor dear Willy, how many more amusements I have than he!"

She bought the best paint-box, and received sixpence in change.

"Is there anything else I can show you?" asked the shopkeeper.

"No, thank you," she replied; and turning to the elder lady, she said, "May we go home at once, mamma? It would take me a long time to choose what I shall spend my sixpence in, and I should like to give Willy his paint-box directly."

"By all means," answered the lady; "we will lose no time; and I will bring you again to spend the sixpence whenever you please."

Without one backward glance toward the beautiful doll, the child tripped away by the side of her companion, looking the brightest and happiest of her kind.

I pondered long upon this circumstance; how long I cannot say, for dolls are unable to measure time, they can only date from any particularly striking epochs. For instance, we can say, "Such an affair happened before I lost my leg;" or, "Such an event took place before my new wig was put on;" but of the intricate divisions known to mortals by the names of hours, days, months, etc., we have no idea.

However, I meditated on the kind little sister during what appeared to me a long but not tedious period, for I was gratified at gaining some insight into the qualities proper to distinguish the human race. Readiness to show kindness, and a prefer-

ence of other's interests to her own, were
virtues which I easily perceived in the
little girl's conduct; but one thing per-
plexed me sadly.   I could not understand
why a doll would not have answered her
kind intentions as well as a paint-box;
why could she not have bought the doll
which she admired so much, and have
given *that* to her brother.

My thoughts were still engaged with
this subject, when a boy approached the
stall. Boys were new characters to me,
and I was glad of the opportunity to ob-
serve one. He did not bestow a look on
the dolls and other toys, but asked for a
box of carpenter's tools. The shopkeeper dived into some hidden recess under the
counter, and produced a clumsy looking
chest, the merits of which I could not discover; but the boy pronounced it to be
" just the thing," and willingly paid down
its price. I followed him with my eyes as
he walked about with his great box under
his arm, looking from side to side, till he
caught sight of another boy rather younger
than himself, advancing from an opposite
corner.

"Why, Geoffrey," exclaimed my first friend, "where have you been all this time? I have been hunting everywhere for you."

Geoffrey did not immediately answer, his mouth being, as I perceived, quite full. When at last he could open his lips, he said, "Will you have a cheese-cake?"

"No, thank you," replied his friend. "We must go home to dinner so soon, that you will scarcely have time to choose your things. Where *have* you been?"

"At the pastry-cook's stall," answered Geoffrey; "and I must go back again before I can buy anything. I left my five shillings there to be changed."

The boys returned together to the stall, and I saw its mistress hand a small coin to Geoffrey.

"Where is the rest?" said he.

"That is your change, sir," she replied.

"Why, you don't mean that those two or three tarts and jellies cost four and sixpence!" he exclaimed, turning as red as the rosiest doll at my side.

"I think you will find it correct, sir," answered the shopkeeper. "Two jellies,

sixpence each, make one shilling; two
custards, sixpence each, two shillings; a
bottle of ginger-beer, threepence, two and
threepence; one raspberry cream, sixpence, two and ninepence; three goose-
berry tarts, threepence, three shillings;
two strawberry tarts, three and two-
pence; two raspberry ditto, three and
fourpence; four cheese-cakes, three and
eightpence; two Bath buns, four shillings;
and one lemon ice, four and sixpence."

"What a bother!" said Geoffrey, as he
pocketed the small remains of his fortune.
"I wish I could give her some of the tarts
back again, for they weren't half so nice
as they looked, except just the first one or
two."

"Because you were only hungry for the
first one or two," said the other boy.
"But it can't be helped now; come and
spend the sixpence better."

"There won't be anything worth buying for sixpence," said Geoffrey gloomily,
as he shuffled in a lazy manner toward my
stall. "I want a spade," said he.

Several were produced, but they cost
two shillings or half a crown. There

were little wooden spades for sixpence;
but from those he turned with contempt,
saying they were only fit for babies.
Nothing at our table suited him, and he
walked toward our opposite neighbor, who
sold books, maps, etc. On his asking for
a dissected map, all the countries of the
world were speedily offered to his choice;
but alas! the price was again the obstacle.
The cheapest map was half a crown; and
Geoffrey's sixpence would buy nothing
but a childish puzzle of Old Mother Hub-
bard. Geoffrey said it was a great shame
that everything should be either dear or
stupid.

"Can't you lend me some money, Ned?"
continued he.

"I can't, indeed," replied the other;
"mine all went in this box of tools. Suppose you don't spend the sixpence at all
now, but keep it till you get some more."

"No, I won't do that; I hate saving my
money." So saying, he wandered from
stall to stall, asking the price of everything, as if his purse was as full as his
stomach.

"How much is that sailor kite?" "Two

shillings, sir."—"How much is that bat?" "Seven and sixpence."—"How much is that wooden box with secret drawer?" "Three shillings."

"How provoking!" he exclaimed. "I want heaps of things, and this stupid sixpence is no good at all."

"It is better than nothing," said Edward. "It is not every day that one's aunt sends one five shillings to spend in the bazaar; and in common times sixpence is not to be despised. After all, there are plenty of things it will buy. Do you want a top?"

"No; I've got four."

"Garden seeds?"

"What is the use of them, when I can't get a spade?"

"Steel pens? You said this morning you could not write with quills."

"I don't like buying those kind of things with my own money."

"A box? Yesterday you wanted a box."

"I don't care for boxes that won't lock, and I can't get one with a lock and key for sixpence."

" A knife ?"

" Sixpenny knives have only one blade;
I want two."

" Sealing-wax? wafers? a penholder?
a paint-box? India-rubber? pencils?"

" Stupid things!"

" A ball? You might have a very good
ball."

" Not a cricket ball; and I don't care
for any other."

" What a particular fellow you are! I
am sure I could always find something to
spend sixpence in. String? One is always wanting string. You may have a
good ball of whipcord."

" These sort of places don't sell it."

" Then, I say again, keep your money
till you want it."

" No, that I'll never do, when I came
on purpose to spend it. After all, the
only thing I can think of," continued
Geoffrey, after a pause, " is to go back to
the pastry-cook's. There was one kind
of tart I did not taste, and perhaps it
would be nicer than the others. I'll give
you one if you like."

" No, thank you; I am much obliged

2

to you all the same; but I won't help you
to spend your money in that way. Don't
buy any more tarts. Come and walk
about; there are plenty more shops to
look at."

They sauntered on, but Geoffrey, by
various turns, worked his way back to the
pastry-cook's; and as no persuasion could
then bring him away, Edward walked off,
not choosing, as he said, to encourage
him.

Presently I saw a tall gentleman enter
the bazaar, and I wondered what he would
buy. I did not then understand the difference between grown-up people and
children, and as he approached my stall,
I could not repress a hope that he would
buy *me*. But his quick eye glanced over
the tables without resting on any of the
toys.

"Can I show you anything, sir?" said
my mistress.

"No, I am much obliged to you," he
answered, with a pleasant smile. "I am
only in search of some young people who,
I dare say, have been better customers
than I. Ah, here they are," he continued,

as the two boys of whom I had taken so much notice ran up to him from different ends of the room.

"Well, boys," said he, "what have you bought? Must we hire a wagon to carry your property home?"

"Not quite," answered Edward. "I have bought a wagon-load of amusement, but I can carry it home well enough myself; I have spent all my money in this box of tools."

"A very sensible and useful purchase," said the gentleman; "they will give you plenty of pleasant employment. The only objection is, that they are likely to be lost or broken at school."

"I do not mean to take them to school, papa. I shall use them in the holidays, and leave them with Willy when I go back to school; that was one reason why I bought them. Willy could do a good deal of carpentering on his sofa."

"True, my boy, and a kind thought. They will be a great amusement to poor Willy, and he will take good care of them for you."

"Now, Geoffrey, how have you invested

your capital? I hope you have found a strong spade. It is fine weather for gardening."

"No, I haven't," stammered Geoffrey.

"Well, what have you bought?"

"I don't know," said Geoffrey.

"Do you mean that you have not spent your money yet? Make haste, then, for I can only allow you five minutes more. I expected to find you ready to go home. Be brisk; there is everything on that stall that the heart of boy can wish," said the gentleman, pointing to my abode.

But Geoffrey did not move. "I don't want anything," said he at last.

"What a fortunate boy!" said the gentleman; but he presently added, "Have you lost your money?"

"No."

"Show it to me."

Geoffrey slowly produced his sixpence, almost hidden in the palm of his hand.

"Where is the rest?" asked the gentleman. "Have you spent it?"

"Yes."

"And nothing to show for it? Nothing?"—and the gentleman looked at the boy more narrowly. "Nothing," said he again, "except a few crumbs of pie-crust on your waistcoat? Oh, Geoffrey!"

There was a short silence, and the boy colored a good deal; at last he said, "It was my own money."

"You will wish it was your own again before long, I dare say," said the gentleman. "However, we must hope you will be wiser in time. Come home to dinner."

"I don't want any dinner," said Geoffrey.

"Probably not, but Edward and I do. We have not dined on tarts; and I dare say Ned is as hungry as I am."

So saying, he led the way towards the door, leaving me, as usual, pondering over what had passed. One word used by the gentleman made a great impression on me—useful.

What could that mean? Various considerations were suggested by the question. Some things, it seemed, were useful, others not; and what puzzled me most was, that the very same things appeared to be useful to some people, and not to others. For instance, the sixpenny paint-

box, which had been rejected as useless
to Willy, was bought soon afterwards by a
small boy, who said it would be the most
useful toy he had.

Could this be the same with everything?

Was it possible that everything prop-
erly applied might have its use, and that
its value depended upon those who used
it? If so, why was Geoffrey blamed for
spending his money in tarts? *He* liked
them. Perhaps he had plenty of food at
home, and that uselessness consisted in a
thing's not being really wanted. I re-
volved the subject in my mind, and tried
to discover the use of everything I saw,
but I was not always successful. The
subject was perplexing; and gradually all
my thoughts became fixed on the point of
most importance to myself—namely, my
own use.

How changed were my ideas since the
time when I imagined the world to belong
to dolls! Their whole race now seemed
to be of very small importance; and as
for my individual self, I could not be sure
that I had any use at all, and still less
what, or *to whom.*

Day after day I lay on my counter un-
noticed, except by the shopwoman who
covered us up at night, and rearranged
us in the morning; and even this she did
with such an indifferent air, that I could
not flatter myself I was of the smallest
use to *her*.

Every necessary care was bestowed
upon me in common with my companions; but I sighed for the tender attentions that I sometimes saw lavished by
children upon their dolls, and wished that
my mistress would nurse and caress me
in the same manner. She never seemed
to think of such a thing. She once said
I was dusty, and whisked a brush over
my face; but that was the only separate
mark of interest I ever received from
her. I had no reasonable ground of com-
plaint, but I began to grow weary of the
insipidity of my life, and to ask myself
whether this could be my only destiny.
Was I never to be of use to anybody?
From time to time other toys were carried
away. Many a giddy top and lively ball
left my side in childish company, and disappeared through those mysterious gates

by which the busy human race entered our
calm seclusion.

At last even dolls had their day.   The
beautiful waxen princess no longer graced
our dominions.   She was bought by an
elderly lady for a birthday present to a
little grand-daughter; and on the very
same day the "old familiar faces" of six
dolls who had long shared my counter
vanished from my sight, one after another
being bought and carried away.   I was
sorry to lose them, though while we had
lived together we had had our little miffs
and jealousies.   I had sometimes thought
that the one with the red shoes was always
sticking out her toes; that she of the flaxen
ringlets was ready to let every breath of
wind blow them over her neighbors' faces;
that another with long legs took up more
room than her share, much to my incon-
venience.   But now that they were all
gone, and I never could hope to see them
again, I would gladly have squeezed myself into as small compass as the baby doll
in the walnut-shell, in order to make room
for them once more.

One thing, however, was satisfactory:

dolls certainly had their use. Seven had been bought, and therefore why not an eighth? I had been sinking almost into a state of despondency, but now my hopes revived and my spirits rose. My turn might come.

And my turn did come. Every circumstance of that eventful day is deeply impressed on my memory. I was as usual employed in making remarks upon the passing crowd, and wondering what might be the use of everybody I saw, when I perceived the lady and the little girl who had been almost my first acquaintances among the human race. As they approached my stall, I heard the mamma say, "Have you decided what to buy with the sixpence?"

"Oh yes, quite," answered the child; "I am going to buy a *sixpenny doll.*"

The words thrilled through me; her eyes seemed fixed on mine, and the sixpence was between her fingers. I imagined myself bought. But she continued: "I think, if you don't mind the trouble, I should like to go round the bazaar first, to see which are the prettiest."

"By all means," replied the lady; and

they walked on, carrying all my hopes with them.

I had often fancied myself the prettiest doll of my size in the place; but such conceit would not support me now. I felt that there were dozens, nay scores, who more than equalled me; and all discontented notions of my neglected merit now sank before the dread that I had really no merit to neglect.

I began also to have some idea of what was meant by time. My past life had glided away so imperceptibly that I did not know whether it had been long or short; but I learned to count every moment while those two mortals were walking round the bazaar.

I strained my eyes to catch sight of them again; but when at last they reappeared, I scarcely dared to look, for fear of seeing a doll in the child's hands. But no; her hands were empty, except for the sixpence still between her finger and thumb.

They came nearer—they stopped at another stall; I could not hear what they said, but they turned away, and once more stood opposite me. The child remained for some moments as silent as myself, and then exclaimed, "After all, mamma, I don't think there are any prettier dolls than these in the whole room."

"What do you say to this one, miss?" said our proprietor, taking up a great full-dressed Dutch doll, and laying her on the top of those of my size and class, completely hiding the poor little victims under her stiff muslin and broad ribbons.

But on the child's answering, "No, thank you, I only want a sixpenny doll not dressed," the Dutch giantess was removed, and we once more asserted our humble claims.

"That seems to be a very pretty one," said the mamma, pointing to my next neighbor. The child for a moment hesitated, but presently exclaimed in a joyful tone, "Oh no! *this* is the beauty of all; this little darling with the real hair and blue ribbon in it; I will take this one, if you please." And before I could be sure that she meant me, I was removed from my place, wrapped up in paper, and consigned to her hands. My long-cherished

wishes were fulfilled, and I was bought.
At first I could scarcely believe it.   Notwithstanding all my planning and looking
forward to this event, now that it really
happened, I could not understand it.   My
senses seemed gone.   What had so long
occupied my mind was the work of a moment; but that moment was irrevocable,
and my fate was decided.   In my little
mistress' hands I passed the boundaries
of the world of toys, and entered upon a
new state of existence.

CHAPTER II.

A VERY different life now opened before me. I had no longer any pretence of complaining of neglect. My young mistress devoted every spare moment to the enjoyment of my company, and set no limits to her caresses and compliments; while I in return regarded her with all the gratitude and affection which a doll can feel. My faculties as well as my feelings were called into fresh exercise; for though I had no longer the wide range of observation afforded by the daily crowd of strangers in the bazaar, I had the new advantage of making intimate acquaintance with a small circle of friends.

Having hitherto been so completely without any position in the world, I could not at first help feeling rather shy at the idea of taking my place as a member of a family; and it was therefore a relief to find that my lot was not cast among total strangers, but that I had already some slight clue to the characters of my future companions.

My mistress, whose name was Rose, was sister to the Willy for whom she had bought the paint-box, and also to Edward, the purchaser of the tools. Geoffrey, the lover of tarts, was a cousin on a visit to them for the holidays; and they had also an elder sister named Margaret, besides their papa and mamma, whom I had seen in the bazaar.

The first of the family to whom I was introduced was Willy, and I soon became much interested in him. He was a pale, thin boy, who spent the day on a sofa, to and from which he was carried in the morning and at night. In fine weather he went out in a wheel-chair; but he was unable to move without help, and was obliged to endure many privations. Though he often looked suffering and weary, he was cheerful and patient, and always seemed pleased to hear other children describe enjoyments in which he could not share. Everybody was fond of Willy, and anxious to amuse and comfort him. All that hap-

pened out of doors was told to him; all
the kindest friends and pleasantest visitors
came to see him; the new books were
brought to him to read first; the best
fruit and flowers set apart for him; and
all the indoor occupations arranged as
much as possible with a view to his con-
venience. He and his little sister Rose
were the dearest friends in the world, and
certain to take part in whatever interested
each other. As soon as Rose brought me
home from the Pantheon she ran upstairs
with me to Willy, whom I then saw for
the first time, sitting on the sofa with
his feet up, and a table before him, on
which stood several books and my old
acquaintances the paint-box and the chest
of tools.

"Look at this, Willy; is not this pretty?"
exclaimed Rose, laying me down on his
open book. Willy looked up with a pleasant smile. "Very pretty," he answered.
"I suppose she is to be the lady of the
new house; and with Ned's tools, I hope
to make some furniture worth her accept-
ance."

"Oh, thank you, Willy dear. And will

you help me to choose a name for her?
What do you think the prettiest name you
know?"

"*Rose*," answered Willy, laughing; "but
I suppose that will not do. I dare say
you want something very fine and out-of-
the-way."

"As fine as can be," replied Rose. "I
have been thinking of Seraphina or Wilhel-
mina: which do you like best?"

"Call it Molly," cried Edward, who
just then entered the room. "Molly and
Betty are the best names: no nonsense in
them."

"Call it Stupid Donkey," mumbled a
voice behind him, and Geoffrey advanced,
his mouth as usual full of something besides words. "Have any nuts, Willy?"
he asked, holding out a handful.

"No, thank you," answered Willy. "I
must not eat them."

"I wouldn't be you, I know," said
Geoffrey, cracking one between his teeth.
"Never let to eat anything but what's
wholesome, and always reading, or doing
something stupid. I believe you are help-
ing Rose to play with that doll now. Put

it into the fire; that is the way to treat dolls. Stupid things. I hate 'em!"

"Pray do not touch it, Geff," said Rose.

"Leave it alone, Geff," said Edward. "You have your things, and Rose has hers. I don't see the fun of dolls myself, but she does, and nobody shall interfere with her while I am here to protect her. Just remember that, will you?"

"The d-o-ll!" said Geoffrey, drawling the word, and making a face as if the pronouncing it turned him quite sick. "Oh, the sweet doll! Perhaps you would like to stay and play with Rose, and Willy and the d-o-ll, instead of coming out to cricket."

"Nonsense, you foolish fellow, you know better," answered Edward. "But I won't have Rose bullied; and what's more, I won't have Willy quizzed. I should like to see you or me pass such an examination as Willy could if he were at school. Why, he can learn as much in a day as we do in a week."

"Well, he is welcome to learn as much as he likes," said Geoffrey; "and let's

3

you and I go and play. What stupid
nuts these are! I've almost cracked one
of my teeth with cracking them."

The boys ran off; and presently there
came into the room the papa and mamma,
whom I already knew, and a young lady
very like Rose, but older. I found she
was Margaret, the eldest sister. They inquired whether Willy wanted anything before they went out; and Margaret fetched
a drawing that he wished to copy, while
his father and mother wheeled his sofa
and table nearer the window, that he might
have more light. When he was made quite
comfortable, they told Rose that she might
stay and take care of him till they returned; and she said she would bring her
box of scraps and begin dressing me.
Then I came in for my share of notice,
and had every reason to be satisfied with
the praises bestowed on me. The mamma said that I deserved very neatly
made clothes; the papa, that my hair
would be a pattern for Margaret's; and
Margaret said I was charming, and that
she would make me a pink satin gown.

They admired the name *Seraphina,*

though her papa suggested various others which he thought might suit Rose's taste —Sophonisba, Cleopatra, Araminta, Dulcinea, Ethelinda, etc.; but as she remained steady to her first choice, the Lady Seraphina was decided to be thenceforth my name and title.

And now began the real business of my life. I was no longer doomed to fret at being of no use, for the object of my existence was plain enough, namely, to give innocent recreation to my young mistress when at leisure from her more serious employments. Every day she spent some hours in study with her mother or sister; and she would fly to me for relief between her lessons, and return to them with more vigor after passing a little time in my refreshing company. She often showed her tasks to me, and discussed their difficulties. I think she repeated the multiplication-table to me nearly a hundred times, while I sat on the "Tutor's Assistant" waiting for the recurrence of the fatal words, "Seven times nine." Day after day she could get no farther; but as soon as she came to "Seven times nine," I was turned off the book, which had to be consulted for the answer.

At last, one day she came running into the room in great glee, exclaiming, " I have done the multiplication-table. I have said it quite right, sixty-three and all. I made no mistake even in dodging. And *you* helped me, my darling Lady Seraphina. I never could have learned it perfect if you had not heard me say it so often. And now, look at your rewards. Margaret has made you a bonnet, and Willy has made you an armchair."

Beautiful, indeed, was the bonnet, and commodious the arm-chair; and I wore the one and reclined in the other all the time Rose was learning the French auxiliary verbs *être* and *avoir*. I flattered myself I was of as much use in them as in the multiplication-table; but I do not recollect receiving any particular recompense. Indeed, after a little time, it would have been difficult to know what to give me, for I possessed everything that a doll's heart could wish, or her head imagine. Such a variety of elegant dresses as Rose made

for me would have been the envy of all
my old friends in the bazaar. I had
gowns of pink satin and white satin; blue
silk and yellow silk; colored muslins without number, and splendid white lace.
Bonnets enough to furnish a milliner's
shop were mine; but I was not so partial
to them as to my gowns, because they
tumbled my hair. I believe a good many
of my possessions were presents from Margaret to Rose on account of perfect lessons; but in course of time I ceased to
superintend Rose's studies. Margaret
said that I interrupted the course of history; and the mamma said that Rose was
old enough to learn her lessons without
bringing her play into them, and that I
must be put away during school hours.

Though I did not think that the fault
was altogether mine, I quite acquiesced
in the wisdom of this decree; for during
Rose's last reading-lesson she had stopped
so often to ask me which I liked best,
Lycurgus or Solon, Pericles or Alcibiades,
etc., that Margaret was almost out of pa-
tience. And though I made no answer,
and had really no choice at all between

the characters, I felt that I rather hindered business.

I was therefore now left to myself for several hours in the morning; but I found ample and pleasant employment in surveying the comforts and beauties of my habitation. For I was not forced to perform the part of an insignificant pigmy in the vast abodes of the colossal race of man: I possessed a beautiful little house proportioned to my size, pleasantly situated on a table in the furthest corner of the school-room, and commanding an extensive view of the whole apartment.

I must describe my house at full length. It had been originally, as I heard, a mere rough packing-case; but what of that? The best brick house in London was once but clay in the fields; and my packing-case was now painted outside and papered inside, and fitted up in a manner every way suitable for the occupation of a doll of distinction.

My drawing-room was charming; light and cheerful, the walls papered with white and gold, and the floors covered with a drab carpet worked with flowers of every

hue. Rose worked the carpet herself under the directions of Margaret, who pre-
vailed upon her to learn worsted-work for
my sake. So there, again, how useful I
was! From the ceiling hung a brilliant
glass chandelier, a birthday-present from
Edward to Rose; and the mantel-piece was
adorned by a splendid mirror cut out of a
broken looking-glass by Willy, and framed
by his hands. I cannot say that Willy ever
seemed to care for me personally, but
he took considerable interest in my up-
holstery, and much of my handsomest
furniture was manufactured by him. He
made my dining-room and drawing-room
tables; the frames of my chairs, which were
covered with silk by Margaret; my sofa,
and my four-post bedstead; and it was he
who painted the floor-cloth in my hall, and
the capital picture of the Queen and Prince
Albert which hung over the dining-room
chimney-piece. I had a snug bed-room,
containing a bed with pink curtains, a toi-
lette-table, with a handsome looking-glass,
pincushion, and rather large brush and
comb; a washing-stand, towel-horse, chest
of drawers, and wardrobe. But the last

two, I must confess, were rather for show
than for use. They were French-polished,
and in appearance convenient as well as
handsome, but in reality too small to hold
my clothes. A few minor articles of dress
were kept in them; but the mass of my
gorgeous attire was always in larger boxes
and trunks belonging to my mistress; her
work-box, for instance, and at one time
her desk; but her mamma turned all my
gowns out of the latter when she banished
me from the lessons, and desired that, for
the future, only writing materials should
be kept in it. "Everything in its proper
place, Rose," I heard her say. "You have
plenty of little boxes for doll's clothes;
and your doll ought to teach you to be
more tidy instead of less so."

My dining-room was well adapted for
all the purposes of hospitality, being furnished with a substantial dining-table,
chairs, and a sideboard, on which there
always stood two trays, one filled with de-
canters and wine-glasses, and the other
with knives and forks. My kitchen was
resplendent with saucepans, kettles, pots
and pans, and plates and dishes, ranged

upon the dresser, or hung from the walls.
A joint of meat was always roasting before
the fire, and a cook of my own race appeared to spend her life in basting it, for
I never failed to find her thus employed
when Rose was so kind as to take me into
my kitchen. There was also a footman,
who sat forever in the hall; and I was inclined to consider him rather wanting in
respect, till I discovered that, owing to a
broken leg, he was unable to stand. I did
not quite comprehend the use of my servants, as Rose herself did all the work of
my house; but she said they were indis-
pensable, and that if it were not for want
of room, I should have a great many
more.

Besides all these arrangements for my
comfort in-doors, I possessed a beautiful
open phaeton, emblazoned with the royal
arms of England, and drawn by four pie-
bald horses with long tails, so spirited that
they never left off prancing. Every day,
after school-time, Rose brought this equi-
page to my door; and the four horses stood
with their eight front feet in the air while
I was dressed for my drive. Then, attired

in my last new bonnet and cloak, I sat in
state in my carriage, and was drawn round
and round the room by Rose, till she said
I was tired.   She made many attempts to
persuade the lame footman to stand on the
footboard behind, but she never could
manage it.   He was a very helpless creature; and I am not quite certain that he
even did his best, little as that might be.
The first time Rose sat him up behind the
carriage, he tumbled head over heels into
the middle of it, and stood there on his
head till she picked him out again.   Then
he fell off behind, then on one side, and
then on the other, till she was quite tired
of his foolish tricks, and left him to sit
quietly and stupidly in his old place in the
hall.

I lived in great comfort in my pleasant
house, and being of a cheerful, contented
temper, never felt lonely, although left to
myself during great part of the day; for
Rose was very obedient to her mamma's
orders, and even if now and then tempted
to forget the regulation herself, Willy was
always at hand to remind her, and help
to fix her attention on her business.   But

when it was all over, she flew to me with
redoubled pleasure.

One day she said to me, " My dear Seraphina, I am afraid you must be very dull,
alone all the morning." I longed to as-
sure her of the contrary; but not having
the gift of speech, I could only listen sub-
missively while she continued: "It is a
pity that you should sit doing nothing
and wasting your time; so I have brought
you some books, which you are to read
while I am at my lessons; and I shall
expect you to learn just as much as I
do."

So saying, she seated me on my sofa,
and placing a table with the books before
me, " Look," continued she, " I have made
them for you myself, and covered them
with these pretty red and green papers.
This is your English History, and this is
your French Grammar; and here is a
Geography book, and here is a History
of Rome. Now read attentively, and do
not let your thoughts wander, and be very
careful not to dogs-ear the leaves; that
alway looks like a dunce. And mind you
sit upright," added she, looking back, as

she left the room in obedience to a summons from her sister.

I obeyed to the best of my power. To be sure, I did not know which was geography and which was grammar, and English and Roman history were both alike to me. But I did as I was bid. I sat upright in the place appointed me, staring as hard as I could at the open pages; and my worst enemy could not accuse me of dogs-earing a single leaf.

When my mistress returned, she pleased me much by calling me a very good girl, and saying that if I continued to take so much pains, I could not fail to improve. On hearing this Willy laughed, and said he hoped that that was a duplicate of Margaret's last speech; and Rose looked very happy, and answered that not only Margaret, but mamma had said the same.

This was not my only duplicate of Rose's adventures. My education appeared to be conducted precisely on the same plan as her own. Before long she brought a little piano-forte and set it up in my drawing-room. I thought it rather hid the pretty paper, but it was a handsome piece of furniture.

"Now, Lady Seraphina," said Rose, " I am going to practise for an hour every day and you must do the same. See what a pretty piano I have given you. You need not mind its being meant for a housewife and pincushion; the notes are marked, and that is all you want. Now practise your scales, and be very careful to strike right notes, and count your time."

I sat at my piano with all due diligence, but I am sorry to say my progress did not seem satisfactory. One day Rose said that she was sure I had forgotten to count; and another day, that I hurried the easy bars and slackened the difficult ones; then she accused me of not caring whether I played right notes or wrong, and torturing her ear by my false chords; then I banged the notes till I broke the strings: in short, there was no end to her complaints, till at last she wound them all up by declaring that both she and I hated music, and that if mamma and Margaret would take her advice, we should both leave it off.

But still I practised regularly, and so, I suppose, did Rose; and gradually her reproaches diminished, and she grew more contented with me; and we both persevered, till she said that really, after all, I seemed to have a good ear, and to be likely to make a very respectable player.

"But you know it all depends upon yourself, Seraphina; your present improvement is the result of pains and practise. Pains and practise will do anything."

It was fortunate for me that I had so careful a superintendent as Rose; for unless she had kept a constant watch over me, there is no saying how many awkward habits I might unconsciously have contracted. But she cured me of poking my head forward, of standing on one leg, of tilting my chair, of meddling with things that were not my own, of leaning against the furniture while I was speaking, of putting my elbows on the table, of biting my nails, of spilling my tea and of making crumbs on the floor.

I cannot say I was myself aware either of the faults or their cure; but I think one seldom does notice one's own faults, and therefore it is a great advantage to

have kind friends who will point them
out to us. I believed Rose when she
told me of mine; so I had a right to believe her when she gave me the agreeable
assurance of their cure, and to indulge the
hope that I was becoming a pleasing,
well-bred little doll.

On one mortifying occasion, however,
I must own that Rose's anxiety for my
always following in her steps was the
cause of a serious injury to me. She re-
marked that I had got into a horrid way
of kicking off my shoes while I was learning my poetry; and she thought the best
cure would be to make me wear sandals.
I observed that she was sewing sandals to
her own shoes at the time, and she consulted Willy about some means of doing
the same by mine. Willy held me head
downwards, and examined my feet. My
shoes were painted, therefore sewing was
out of the question. He advised glue.
This was tried, but it came through the
thin narrow ribbon of which my sandals
were to be made, and looked very dirty.
They were taken off, but the operation
had spoiled the delicacy of my white

stockings, and Rose said it was impossible
to let me go such an untidy figure; we
must try some other way.   She asked
Willy to lend her a gimlet, that she might
bore holes at the sides of my feet, and glue
the ribbon into them, so as not to show
the glue.   Willy said she was welcome to
the gimlet, but that he desired her to
leave it alone, for that she would only
break my feet.   But Rose would not be
dissuaded, and began boring.   It was on
this occasion that I most peculiarly felt
the advantage of that insensibility to pain
which distinguishes my race.   What mortal could have borne such an infliction
without struggling and screaming?   I, on
the contrary, took it all in good part, and
showed no signs of feeling even at the
fatal moment when my foot snapped in
two, and Rose, with a face of utter dismay held up my own toes before my eyes.

"O, my poor Seraphina!" she exclaimed, "what shall we do?"

"Glue it on again," said Willy.   "You
had better have taken my advice at first,
but now you must make the best of it.
Glue is your only friend."

So Rose glued the halves of my foot together, lamenting over me, and blaming herself so much all the time, that it seemed rather a comfort to her when Margaret, coming into the room, agreed with her that she had been foolish and awkward. Margaret said that ribbon might have been tied over my feet from the first, without using glue or gimlet either; and Rose called herself more stupid than ever, for not having thought of such an easy contrivance.

My foot was glued, and for the purpose of standing answered as well as ever; and Rose sewed me up in a pair of blue silk boots, and declared that I was prettier than before; and my misfortune was soon forgotten by everybody but myself. I, however, could not but feel a misgiving that this was the first warning of my share in the invariable fate of my race. For I had already lived long enough to be aware that the existence of a doll has its limits. Either by sudden accidents, such as loss of limbs, or by the daily wear and tear of life, decay generally makes its progress in us, and we fade

4

away as surely as the most delicate of the fragile race of mortals.

Though the fracture of my foot was my own first misfortune, I had had opportunities of remarking the casualties to which dolls are liable. For it is not to be supposed that our devotion to human beings precludes us from cultivating the society of our own species. Dolls will be dolls; and they have a natural sympathy with each other, notwithstanding the companionship of the race of man. Most little girls are aware of this fact, and provide suitable society for their dolls. I myself had a large circle of silent acquaintances, to whom I was introduced by Rose's kindness and consideration. When other little girls came to drink tea with her, they often brought their dolls to spend the evening with me; and among them I had more than once the pleasure of recognizing an old friend from the bazaar.

Then I was in my glory. There was a constant supply of provisions in my larder; and at a moment's notice Rose would produce an excellent dinner, all

ready cooked, and dished in a beautiful
little china dinner-service. Willy compared her to the genius of Aladdin's lamp;
and though I did not know what that
might mean, I quite understood the advantage of being able to set such a ban-
quet before my friends. I could always
command salmon, a pair of soles, a leg of
mutton, a leg of pork, a turkey, a pair of
boiled fowls, a ham, a sucking pig, a hare,
a loaf of bread, a fine Cheshire cheese,
several pies, and a great variety of fruit,
which was always ripe and in season,
winter or summer. Rose's papa once observed that his hot-house produced none
so fine; for the currants were as large as
apples, and two cherries filled a dish.

Rose and her companions performed
the active duties of waiting at table on
these occasions; but the lame footman was
generally brought out of the hall and
propped up against the sideboard, where
he stood looking respectable but awkward.

At these pleasant parties I saw a great
range of characters, for Rose's young
visitors were various in their tastes, and
their dolls used to be dressed in every

known costume.   Besides plenty of pretty
English damsels, I was introduced now to
a Turkish sultana, now to a Swiss peas-
ant; one day to a captain in the British
army, another day to an Indian rajah.
One young lady liked to make her dolls
personate celebrated characters; and when
she visited us, most distinguished guests
graced my table.   I have had the honor
of receiving the Queen and Prince Albert
themselves; the Duke of Wellington, Sir
Walter Scott, and Miss Edgeworth have
all dined with me on the same day, and
Robinson Crusoe came in the evening.

But it was at these social meetings that
I became most fully aware of the liability
of dolls to loss of limbs.   I never remember giving a party at which the guests
could boast of possessing all their legs and
arms.   Many an ingenious contrivance
hid or supplied the deficiencies, and we
were happy in spite of our losses; still,
such was the case: and I saw that dolls,
however beloved and respected, could not
last forever.

For some time after my accident I had
no particular adventures.   I lived in

peace and plenty, and amused myself with watching the family. They were all amiable and easy to understand, except Geoffrey; but he was a complete puzzle to me, and it was long before I could make out why he was so different from the rest.

The others all seemed to like to help and please one another, but Geoffrey never seemed happy unless he was making himself disagreeable. If Willy was interested in a book, he was obliged to sit upon the second volume, or Geoffrey would be sure to run away with it.

If Edward was in a hurry to go out, Geoffrey would hide his cap, and keep him a quarter of an hour hunting for it. The girls dared not leave their worsted work within his reach for a moment, for he would unravel the canvas, or chop up the wool, or go on with the work after a pattern of his own composing, so that they would be obliged to spend a half an hour in unpicking his cobbling.

Margaret remonstrated with him in private, and made excuses for him in public, and did her best to prevent his tiresome tricks from annoying Willy; Edward tried rougher means of keeping him in order, which sometimes succeeded; but still he could find plenty of opportunities of being a torment: people always can when such is their taste.

One day Margaret was keeping Willy company, while the rest of the party were gone to the Zoölogical Gardens. She had brought a drawing to finish, as he liked to see her draw, and was sometimes useful in suggesting improvements. But while they were thus employed, Margaret was summoned to some visitors, and went away, saying that her drawing would just have time to dry before she returned.

But, unfortunately, during her absence, Geoffrey came home. He had grown tired of the Gardens, which he had seen very often, and rather hungry, as he generally was; so after amusing himself by eating the cakes he had bought for the bear, he had nothing more to do, and tried to persuade his cousins to be tired also. But Edward was making himself agreeable to the monkeys, Rose was cultivating the friendship of the elephant,

and their papa and mamma were waiting
to see the hippopotamus bathe; so that
Geoffrey's proposals of leaving the Gardens were scouted, and he could only obtain leave from his uncle to go home by
himself.

He entered the room, as usual, with
his mouth full, having spent his last penny
in a piece of cocoanut as he came along
the streets. While the cocoanut lasted,
he was employed to his satisfaction; but
when that was finished, he was again at a
loss for something to do. He tried walking round the room on one leg, working
heel and toe, and that succeeded very
well, and did no harm till he unluckily
came to the drawing-table, when he immediately brought himself to a stand on
both feet.

"Hallo!" cried he, "here's a daub!
Is this your splendid performance, Will?"

"No," replied Willy, "it is Margaret's;
and mind you don't touch it by accident,
because it is wet."

"Touch it by accident!" exclaimed
Geoffrey. "I am going to touch it on
purpose. I wonder Margaret is not

ashamed to do it so badly.   I'll improve
it for her.   How kind of me!"

Poor Willy, in dismay, tried to secure
the drawing, but he could not move from
his sofa, and Geoffrey danced round him,
holding it at arm's-length.

Then Willy caught at the bell-rope, but
his mischievous cousin snatched it quicker,
and tied it up out of his reach.   Willy
called all the servants as loud as he could,
but no one was within hearing, and he
threw himself back on his sofa in despair,
exclaiming, "How can you be so ill-natured, when Margaret is always so kind
to you?"

"Ill-natured!" answered the other;
"I'm doing her a favor.   She admired
the moonlight in the Diorama; now I
shall make just such a moon in her drawing."   And while he spoke, a great yellow moon, like a guinea, rose in the midst
of poor Margaret's brilliant sunset.

"That's the thing," said Geoffrey;
"and now I shall put the cow jumping over
it, and the little dog laughing to see such
sport.   Some figures always improve the
foreground."

"Oh, you have quite spoiled it!" cried
Willy. "How I wish I could stop you!
I cannot imagine how you can like to be
so mischievous and disagreeable. Oh, if
Margaret would but come back!"

At last Margaret came, and the trouble-
some Geoffrey expected great amusement
from her displeasure; but he was disappointed. Margaret was one of those
generous people who never resent an injury done to themselves. If Geoffrey had
spoiled anybody else's drawing, she would
have been the first to punish him; but
now she was much more vexed at Willy's
distress than at the destruction of her
own work, and instead of scolding Geoffrey she gave herself up to consoling
Willy. She assured him that there was
no great harm done. She said the drawing was good for very little, and that she
would copy it and improve it so much
that he should be quite glad of the dis-
aster; and she made a present of the
spoiled drawing to Geoffrey, telling him
she was sure he would one day be ashamed
of so foolish a performance, but that
meanwhile he might keep it as a specimen

of his taste.   He had not the manners to
apologize, but he looked very silly and
crest-fallen, and left the room in silence,
with the drawing in his hand.

When he was gone, Willy exclaimed,
"If it were not for losing Edward, I
should wish the holidays were over;
Geoffrey is so disagreeable."

"He is very thoughtless," Margaret replied; "but we must not be too hard upon
him.   Let us recollect that he has no
parents to teach him better, nor brothers
and sisters to call forth his consideration
for others.   Poor Geoffrey has had neither
example nor precept till now.   But now
Papa and Mamma give him good precepts;
and if we try to set him good examples,
perhaps we may help him to improve."

"Well, I'll hope for the best, and do
what I can," said Willy.   "Certainly he
has some good qualities.   He is as brave
as a lion; and he is good-natured about
giving away his own things, though he
is so mischievous with other people's."

"And he is clever in his way, notwithstanding his idleness," added Margaret.
"Those foolish figures that he put into

my drawing were uncommonly well done, though they were provoking to us."

"You are the best girl in the world," said Willy; "and if you think Geoffrey will improve, I'll think so too; but you must own there is room for it."

Perhaps Geoffrey did improve, but it seemed slow work, faults being more easily acquired than cured; and for a long time I could perceive no difference in him. Indeed, as his next piece of mischief concerned myself, I thought him worse than ever.

I have often wondered at the extreme dislike which boys have to dolls. I was the most inoffensive creature possible, giving myself no airs, and interfering with nobody; yet even the gentle Willy was indifferent to me.

Edward, though he protected Rose in her patronage to me, despised me thoroughly himself; and Geoffrey never lost an opportunity of expressing his mortal hatred to me. I shrank from Edward's contemptuous notice, but I was not at all afraid of him, well knowing that neither he nor Willy would hurt a hair of my head; but whenever Geoffrey came into the room, terror seized my mind. He never passed my house without making all kinds of ugly faces at me; and I felt instinctively that nothing but the presence of the other boys restrained him from doing me any harm in his power.

I had hitherto never been alone with him, but at last the fatal moment arrived. One fine afternoon, Willy went out for a drive in his wheel-chair, Edward insisting upon drawing it himself, and the two girls walking on each side. Geoffrey accompanied them, intending to walk with them part of the way, and to go on by himself when he was tired of the slow pace of the chair. All seemed safe, and I hoped to enjoy a few hours of uninterrupted leisure. I always liked having my time to myself; and as Rose had set me no lessons, I reposed comfortably in my arm-chair by a blazing fire of black and red cloth, from the glare of which I was sheltered by a screen. My dog sat at my side, my cat lay at my feet, and I was as happy as a doll could be.

Suddenly the silence was broken by a

sound as of a turkey gobbling in the hall;
presently this changed to a duck quack-
ing on the stairs; then a cock crew on
the landing-place, and a goose hissed
close to the school-room door. I guessed
but too well what these ominous sounds
portended, and my heart sank within me
as the door burst open and my dreaded
enemy banged into the room.

"Why, they have not come home yet!"
exclaimed he; "so my talents have been
wasted. I meant to have made them bid
me not make every different noise. When
they said, 'Don't hiss,' I would have
crowed; and when they said, 'Don't
crow,' I would have quacked, or barked,
or bellowed, or mewed, till I had gone
through all the noises I know. Now I
have nothing to do."

He walked to the window and looked
out.

"What a stupid street it is!" said he.
"If my uncle had not taken away my
squirt, I would squirt at the people."

Then he yawned, and sauntered to the
bookcase. "What stupid books! I
wonder anybody can write them. I wish

Edward had left his tools out; I should like to plane the top of the shelf.   How stupid it is having nothing to do!"

As he spoke, I shuddered to see him approaching my end of the room.   He came nearer; he made a full stop in front of me, and looked me in the face.

" You stupid, ugly thing," he exclaimed, " don't stare so.   I hate to have a doll's eyes goggling at me."

Gladly would I have withdrawn my eyes, if possible.   But they had been painted wide open, and what could I do? I never was so ashamed of them in my life; but I had no control over them, so I stared on, and he grew more indignant.

" If you don't leave off," he cried, " I'll poke out your eyes, as I did those of the ugly picture in my room.   I won't be stared at."

I longed for the gift of speech, to represent to him that if he would but leave off looking at me I should give him no offence; but alas, I was silent, and could only stare as hard as ever.

" Oh, you will, will you?" said he, " then I know what I'll do: I'll hang you."

In vain I hoped for the return of the rest of the party. I listened anxiously for every sound, but no friendly step or voice was near, and I was completely in his power.

He began rummaging his pockets, grinning and making faces at me all the time. Presently he drew forth a long piece of string, extremely dirty, looking as if it had been trailed in the mud.

"Now for it," he exclaimed; "now you shall receive the reward of all your stupidity and affectation. I do think dolls are the most affected creatures on the face of the earth."

He laid hold of me by my head, pushing my wig on one side. Alas for my beautiful hair, it was disarranged forever. But that was a trifle compared with what followed. He tied one end of his muddy string round my neck, drawing it so tight that I foresaw I should be marked for life, and hung the other end to a nail in the wall.

There I dangled, while he laughed and quizzed me, adding insult to injury. He twisted the string as tight as possible,

and then let it whirl round and round till
it was all untwisted again. I banged
against the wall as I spun like a top, and
wished that I could sleep like a top too.
But I was wide awake to my misfortunes;
and each interval of stillness, when the
string was untwisted, only enhanced them,
by showing in contrast the happy home
whence I had been torn. For I was
hung on the wall directly opposite my own
house; and from my wretched nail I could
distinguish every room in it. Between
my twirls, I saw my pretty drawing-room,
with its comfortable arm-chair now
vacant; and my convenient kitchen, with
my respectable cook peacefully basting
her perpetual mutton. I envied even my
lame footman quietly seated in his chim-
ney-corner, and felt that I had never
truly valued the advantages of my home
till now. Would they ever be restored to
me? Should I once again be under the
protection of my kind and gentle mistress,
or was I Geoffrey's slave forever?

These melancholy thoughts were interrupted by a step on the stairs. "Hallo!"
cried Geoffrey, "who would have thought

of their coming home just now?" and he was going to lift me down from my nail; but when the door opened, the housemaid came in alone, and he changed his mind.

"Why, Master Geoffrey," said she, "what are you doing here all alone? Some mischief, I'll be bound."

"Bow, bow, bow," answered he, dancing and playing all sorts of antics to prevent her seeing me.

"Come," said she, "those tricks won't go down with me. The more lively you are, the more I know you've been after something you ought to have let alone."

"Hee haw, hee haw," said Geoffrey, twitching her gown, and braying like a donkey.

"Well, you're speaking in your own voice at last," said she laughing. "But let go of my gown, if you please: you are big enough to walk by yourself, and I want to set the room to rights. There's some young ladies coming to tea with Miss Rose."

She bustled about, dusting and putting everything in order, and talking all the time, partly to Geoffrey and partly to her-

self, about the blacks that came in at the
windows and made a place want dusting
a dozen times a day, when her eye fell on
my unfortunate figure, which my per-
secutor had just set swinging like the
pendulum of a clock.   I was a deplorable
object.   He had forced me into the most
awkward attitude he could invent.   My
arms were turned round in their sockets,
one stretched toward the ceiling, the other
at full length on one side.   I was forced
to kick one leg out in front and the other
behind; and my knees were bent up the
wrong way.   My wig had fallen off altogether from my head, and was now
perched upon my toe.   I was still swinging when Sarah caught sight of me.   She
looked at me for a moment, and then
turned round opening her eyes at Geoffrey
much wider than I had ever done.

"Why, you audacious, aggravating
boy!" she exclaimed, making a dash at
him with her duster; but he ran away
laughing, and she was obliged to finish
the rest of her speech to herself.

"To think of his being so mischievous
and ill-natured!   What will poor Miss

Rose say? To be sure there is nothing
boys won't do; their equals for perverse-
ness don't walk the earth. Though I
ought not to speak against them, while
there's Master William and Master Edward to contradict me. They are boys,
to be sure; but as for that Geoffrey!"
And here she shook her head in silence,
as if Geoffrey's delinquencies were beyond
the power of words to express. She then
released me; and after restoring my limbs
to their proper position, and smoothing
my discomposed dress, she laid me gently
on my bed, and placed my wig on my
pillow beside me, with many kind expres-
sions of pity and good-will.

Repose was indeed needful after so
agitating an adventure; and I was glad
to be left quiet till the young people came
in from their walk. I composed my
ruffled spirits as well as I could; but I
found it impossible not to be nervous at
the idea of Rose's first seeing me in such
a plight, and I anxiously awaited her return. They came in at last, Rose, Willy,
and Margaret; and after establishing
Willy on his sofa, Rose's next care was to

visit me. "O Willy! O Margaret!" she exclaimed, and burst into tears.

"What is the matter, my darling?" asked Margaret.

Rose could not answer; but Sarah was there to tell the story, and do ample justice to my wrongs. Yet I could not help observing, in the midst of all her indignation, the difference of her manner towards her present hearers and towards Geoffrey. She never seemed on familiar terms with Willy, much less with Margaret or Rose. She neither cut jokes nor used rough language to them, but treated them with the respect due to her master's children; though, as I well knew, she was extremely fond of them, and disliked Geoffrey, in spite of her familiarity with him.

I saw Geoffrey no more that day. Rose's young friends soon arrived, and consoled both her and me by their kind sympathy and attentions. One made an elegant cap to supply the loss of my wig; another strung a blue necklace to hide the black mark round my throat; Rose herself put me to bed, and placed a table by my bedside covered with teacups, each, she told me, containing a different medicine; and the young lady who had once brought Miss Edgeworth to dine with me charged me to lie still and read "Rosamond" till I was quite recovered.

Next morning, as I lay contentedly performing my new part of an invalid, I heard a confidential conversation between Margaret and Geoffrey, in which I was interested.

They were alone together, and she was taking the opportunity to remonstrate with him on his unkind treatment of me.

"What was the harm?" said Geoffrey. "A doll is nothing but wood or bran, or some stupid stuff; it can't feel."

"Of course," answered Margaret, "we all know *that*. It is wasteful and mischievous to spoil a pretty toy; but I am not speaking now so much for the sake of the doll as of Rose. Rose is not made of any stupid stuff; *she* can feel. And what is more, she can feel for other people as well as herself. She would never play such an ill-natured trick."

"I should not mind it if she did," argued Geoffrey; "I am not such a baby."

"You would not mind that particular thing," answered Margaret, "because you do not care about dolls; but you would mind her interfering with *your* pleasure, or injuring your property. You would think it very ill-natured, for instance, if she threw away that heap of nuts which you have hoarded like a squirrel on your shelf of the closet."

"Nuts are not nonsense like dolls," said he. "Besides, she may have as many of mine as she likes. I tried to make her eat some yesterday."

"Yes, and half choked her by poking them into her mouth, when she told you she did not want them. She cares no more for nuts than you do for dolls. You would think it no kindness if she teased you to nurse her doll."

"I should think not, indeed," answered Geoffrey, indignant at the very idea.

"Of course not. Kindness is not shown by forcing our own pleasures down other people's throats, but by trying to promote theirs. That is really doing what we should be done by."

"But doing as we would be done by is one's *duty*," said Geoffrey.

"I fear it is a duty of which you seldom think," replied his cousin.

"Why, one can't be thinking of *duty* in those kind of things," answered he.

"Why not?" asked Margaret.

"Because they are such trifles; duties are great things."

"What sort of things do you consider to be duties?" Margaret inquired.

"Oh, such things as letting one's self be tortured, like Regulus; or forgiving an enemy who has shot poisoned arrows at one, like Cœur de Lion."

"Well," said Margaret, smiling, "such heroic duties as those do not seem likely to fall in your way just now, perhaps they never may. Our fellow-creatures are so kind to us, that we are seldom called upon to fulfil any but small duties towards them, or what you would consider such; for I cannot allow any duty to be small, especially that of doing as we would be done by. If we do not fulfil that in trifles, we

shall probably never fill it at all.   This
is a serious thought, Geoffrey."

Geoffrey looked up; and as he seemed
inclined to listen, Margaret continued
talking to him kindly but gravely, bringing many things before his mind as duties
which he had hitherto considered to be
matters of indifference.   But Margaret
would not allow anything to be a trifle in
which one person could give pain or
pleasure, trouble or relief, annoyance to
another, or by which any one's own mind
or habits could be either injured or im-
proved.   She maintained that there was a
right and a wrong to everything, and that
right and wrong could never be trifles,
whether in great things or small.   By degrees the conversation turned upon matters far too solemn to be repeated by a
mere plaything like myself; but I thought,
as I heard her, that it might be better to
be a poor wooden figure which could do
neither right nor wrong, than a human
being who neglected his appointed duties.

Geoffrey said little, but he shook hands
with Margaret when she had finished
speaking, and I noticed from that day

forward a gradual improvement in his conduct. Bad habits are not cured in a minute, and he did not become all at once as gentle and considerate as Willy, nor as kind and helpful as Edward; but he put himself in the right road, and seemed in a fair way of overtaking them in due time. He at once left off *active* mischief; and if he could not avoid being actually trouble-some, he at any rate cured himself of teasing people on purpose. And it was remarkable how many employments he found as soon as his mind was disengaged from mischief. Instead of his dawdling about all the morning calling things stupid, and saying he had nothing to do, all man-ner of pleasant occupations seemed to start up in his path, as if made to order for him, now that he had time to attend to them. When he relinquished the pleasure of spoiling things, he acquired the far greater pleasure of learning to make them. When Edward was no longer afraid of trusting him with his tools, it was wonderful what a carpenter he turned out. When Margaret could ven-ture to leave drawing materials within his

reach, he began to draw capitally. Good-
natured Margaret gave him lessons, and
said she would never wish for a better
scholar. He found it was twice the
pleasure to walk or play with Edward
when he was thought an acquisition instead of a burden; and far more agreeable
to have Rose and Willy anxious for his
company than wishing to get rid of him.
But the advantages were not confined to
himself; the whole house shared in them;
for his perpetual small annoyances had
made everybody uncomfortable, whereas
now, by attention to what he used to look
upon as trifles, he found he had the power
of contributing his part towards the happiness of his fellow-creatures, which is no
trifle.

On the last day of the holidays, the
young people were all assembled in the
schoolroom till it was time for Edward
and Geoffrey to start. While Edward
was arranging various matters with Willy,
I heard Geoffrey whisper to Margaret that
he hoped she had forgiven him for spoiling that drawing of hers. She seemed at
first really not to know what he meant;

but when she recollected it, she answered
with a smile, "Oh, my dear Geoffrey, I
had forgiven and forgotten it long ago.
Pray never think of it again yourself."

Geoffrey next went up to Rose and put
a little parcel into her hands. On opening it, she found a box of very pretty
bon-bons in the shape of various vege-
tables. When she admired them, he
seemed much pleased, and said that he
had saved up his money to buy them, in
hopes she might like them for her doll's
feasts. Rose kissed and thanked him,
and said she only wished he could stay
and help her and her dolls to eat them.
Everybody took an affectionate leave of
Geoffrey, and Willy said he was very
sorry to lose him, and should miss him
sadly.

Edward and Geoffrey returned to
school, and I never saw Geoffrey again;
but a constant correspondence was kept
up between him and his cousins, and I
often heard pleasant mention of his progress and improvement.

Time passed on; what length of time I
cannot say, all seasons and their change

being alike to me; but schooldays and
holidays succeeded one another, and our
family grew older in appearance and
habits. Rose gradually spent less time
with me, and more with her books and
music, till at last, though she still kept
my house in order, she never actually
played with me, unless younger children
came to visit her, and *then*, indeed, I was
as popular as ever. But on a little friend's
one day remarking that I had worn the
same gown for a month, Rose answered
that she herself had the charge of her
own clothes now, and that what with
keeping them in order, and doing fancy-
work as presents for her friends, she found
no time to work for dolls.

By and by, her time for needlework was
fully engaged in Geoffrey's behalf. He
was going to sea; and Rose was making
purses, slippers, portfolios, and everything she could think of as likely to please
him. Perhaps *her* most useful keepsake
was a sailor's housewife; but many nice
things were sent him from every one of the
family. I saw a trunk full of presents
packed and sent off. And when I recol-

lected my first acquaintance with him, I could not but marvel over the change that had taken place, before books, drawing materials, and mathematical instruments could have been chosen as the gifts best suited to his taste.

Edward used to come home from school as merry and good-humored as ever, and growing taller and stronger every holiday. Rose and Margaret were as flourishing as he; but poor Willy grew weaker, and thinner, and paler. Fresh springs and summers brought him no revival, but as they faded he seemed to fade with them. He read more than ever; and his sisters were frequently occupied in reading and writing under his direction, for they were anxious to help him in his pursuits. His Papa and Mamma sometimes said he studied too hard; and they used to sit with him, and try to amuse him by conversation, when they wished to draw him from his books. Doctors visited him, and prescribed many remedies; and his Mamma gave him all the medicines herself, and took care that every order was implicitly obeyed. His father carried him up and

down stairs, and waited upon him as
tenderly as even Margaret; but he grew
no better with all their care. He was always gentle and patient, but he appeared
in less good spirits than formerly. He
seemed to enjoy going out in his wheel-
chair more than anything; but one day he
observed that the summer was fast coming to an end, and that then he must shut
himself up in his room, for that he minded
the cold more than he used.

"I wish we lived in a warmer country,"
said Rose; "perhaps then you might get
better."

"I do not know about *living*," replied
Willy. "England is the best country to
live in; but I certainly should like to be
out of the way of the cold for this next
winter."

"Why do you not tell Papa so?" asked
Rose.

"Because I know very well he would
take a journey directly, however incon-
venient it might be to him."

Rose said nothing more just then, but
she took the first opportunity of telling
her father what had passed; and he said

he was very glad indeed that she had let him know.

From that day forward something more than usual seemed in contemplation. Papa, Mamma, and Margaret were constantly consulting together, and Edward, Rose, and Willy followed their example. As for me, nobody had time to bestow a look or a thought upon me; but I made myself happy by looking at and thinking of them.

One morning two doctors together paid Willy a long visit. After they were gone, his Papa and Mamma came into the room.

"Well, my boy," his father exclaimed in an unusually cheerful tone, "it is quite settled now; Madeira is the place, and I hope you like the plan."

"Oh, papa," said Willy, "is it really worth while?"

"Of course it is worth while, a hundred times over," replied his father; "and we will be off in the first ship."

"The doctors strongly advise it, and we have all great hopes from it, my dear Willy," said his mother.

"Then so have I," said Willy; "and,

indeed, I like it extremely, and I am very
grateful to you. The only thing I mind
is, that you and my father should have to
leave home and make a long sea voyage,
when you do not like travelling, and Papa
has so much to keep him in England."

"Oh, never mind me," said his mother;
"I shall like nothing so well as travelling
if it does you good."

"And never mind me," said his father;
"there is nothing of so much consequence
to keep me in England, as your health to
take me out of it."

"Besides, my dear child," said his
mother, "as the change of climate is so
strongly recommended for you, it becomes
a duty as well as a pleasure to try it."

"So make your mind easy, my boy,"
added his father; "and I will go and take
our passage for Madeira."

The father left the room, and the mother
remained conversing with the sick child,
whose spirits were unusually excited. I
scarcely knew him again. He was generally slow and quiet, and rather despond-
ing about himself; but he now thought he
should certainly get well, and was so eager

and anxious to start without delay, that
his mother had some difficulty in reconciling him to the idea that no ship would sail
till next month. She also took great pains
to impress upon him the duty of resigna-
tion, in case the attempt should fail, after
all, in restoring his health; and she finally
left him not less hopeful, but more calm
and contented with whatever might befall
him.

And now began the preparations for the
voyage. There was no time to spare,
considering all that had to be done.
Everybody was at work; and though poor
Willy himself could not do much to help,
he thought of nothing else. His common
books and drawings were changed for
maps and voyages; the track to Madeira
was looked up by him and Rose every
day, and sometimes two or three times in
the day, and every book consulted that
contained the least reference to the Madeira Isles.

Edward was an indefatigable packer.
He was not to be one of the travellers, as
his father did not choose to interrupt his
school-education; but no one was more ac-

6

tive than he in forwarding the preparations for the voyage, and no one more
sanguine about its results.

"We shall have Willy back," he would
say, "turned into a fine strong fellow, as
good a cricketer as Geoffrey or I, and a
better scholar than either of us."

Margaret and Rose were to go; and
Rose's young friends all came to take
leave of her, and talk over the plan, and
find Madeira on the map, and look at views
of the island, which had been given to
Willy. And a sailor friend, who had been
all over the world, used to come and
describe Madeira as one of the most
beautiful of all the beautiful places he
had visited, and tell of its blue sea,
fresh and bright, without storms; its high
mountains, neither barren nor bleak; and
its climate, so warm and soft, that Willy
might sit out all day in the beautiful
gardens under hedges of fragrant gera-
niums. And when Willy talked of enjoying the gardens while his younger sisters
were climbing the hills, there was more
to be told of cradles borne upon men's
shoulders, in which Willy could be carried

to the top of the highest hills as easily as
his sisters on their mountain ponies. And
now the packing was all finished, and the
luggage sent on board, and everybody
was anxious to follow it; for the ship was
reported as quite comfortable, and the
house was decidedly the reverse. Margaret and her father had been on board
to arrange the cabins, accompanied by
their sailor-friend, who professed to know
how to fit up a berth better than anybody.
He had caused all the furniture to be
fastened, or, as he called it, *cleated* to the
floor, that it might not roll about in rough
weather. The books were secured in the
shelves by bars, and swinging-tables hung
from the ceilings. Willy's couch was in
the most airy and convenient place at the
stern cabin window, and there was an
easy-chair for him when he should be able
to come out on deck. The ship was said
to be in perfect order, whereas the house
was in the utmost confusion and desola-
tion; the carpets rolled up, the pictures
taken down, the mirrors covered with
muslin, the furniture and bookcases with
canvas; not a vestige left of former

habits and occupations except me and my little mansion. But in the midst of all the bustle, I was as calm and collected as if nothing had happened. I sat quietly in my arm-chair, staring composedly at all that went on, contented and happy, though apparently forgotten by everybody. Indeed, such was my placid, patient disposition, that I do not believe I should have uttered a sound or moved a muscle if the whole of London had fallen about my little ears.

I did certainly sometimes wish to know what was to become of me, and at last that information was given me.

The night before they sailed, Rose busied herself with Sarah in packing up my house and furniture, which were to be sent to a little girl who had long considered it her greatest treat to play with them. But Rose did not pack me up with my goods and chattels.

" My poor old Seraphina," said she, as she removed me from my arm-chair, " you and I have passed many a happy day together, and I do not like to throw you away as mere rubbish; but the new mis-

tress of your house has already more dolls
than she knows what to do with. You
are no great beauty now, but I wish I
knew any child that would care for you."

"If you please to give her to me, Miss
Rose," said Sarah, "my little niece, that
your Mamma is so kind as to put to school,
would thank you kindly, and think her
the greatest of beauties."

"Oh, then, take her by all means,
Sarah," replied Rose; "and here is a little trunk to keep her clothes in. I remember I used to be very fond of that
trunk; so I dare say your little Susan will
like it, though it is not quite new."

"That she will, and many thanks to
you, miss. Susan will be as delighted
with it now as you were a year or two
ago."

So they wrapped me up in paper, and
Rose having given me a farewell kiss,
which I would have returned if I could,
Sarah put me and my trunk both into her
great pocket; and on the same day that
my old friends embarked for their distant
voyage, I was carried to my new home.

CHAPTER III.

A ND now began a third stage of my existence, and a fresh variety of life.

I at first feared that I should have great difficulty in reconciling myself to the change; and my reflections in Sarah's dark pocket were of the most gloomy cast. I dreaded poverty and neglect. How should I, accustomed to the refinements of polished life and the pleasures of cultivated society, endure to be tossed about with no home of my own, and perhaps no one who really cared for me? I knew that I was not in my first bloom, and it seemed unlikely that a new acquaintance should feel towards me like my old friend Rose, who had so long known my value. Perhaps I might be despised; perhaps allowed to go ragged, perhaps even dirty! My spirits sank, and had I been human, I should have wept. But cheerful voices

aroused me from this melancholy reverie,
and I found myself restored to the pleasant
light in the hands of a good-humored-
looking little girl, whose reception of me
soon banished my fears. For, although
altered since the days of my introduction
to the world in the bazaar, so that my
beauty was not quite what it had been, I
still retained charms enough to make me
a valuable acquisition to a child who
had not much choice of toys, and my disposition and manners were as amiable and
pleasing as ever. My new mistress and I
soon loved each other dearly; and in her
family I learned that people might be
equally happy and contented under very
different outward circumstances.

Nothing could well be more unlike my
former home than that to which I was
now introduced. Susan, my little mistress, was a child of about the same age
as Rose when she first bought me; but
Susan had no money to spend in toys, and
very little time to play with them, though
she enjoyed them as much as Rose herself. She gave me a hearty welcome;
and though she could offer me no furnished

house, with its elegances and comforts, she assigned me the best place in her power—the corner of a shelf on which she kept her books, slate, needlework, and inkstand. And there I lived, sitting on my trunk, and observing human life from a new point of view. And though my dignity might appear lowered in the eyes of the unthinking, I felt that the respectability of my character was really in no way diminished; for I was able to fulfil the great object of my existence as well as ever, by giving innocent pleasure, and being useful in my humble way.

No other dolls now visited me; but I was not deprived of the enjoyments of inanimate society, for I soon struck up an intimate acquaintance with an excellent Pen in the inkstand by my side, and we passed our leisure hours very pleasantly in communicating to each other our past adventures. His knowledge of life was limited, having resided in that inkstand, and performed all the writing of the family, ever since he was a quill. But his experience was wise and virtuous; and he could bear witness to many an industrious

effort at improvement, in which he had
been the willing instrument; and to many
a hard struggle for honesty and independence, which figures of his writing had re-
corded. I liked to watch the good Pen
at his work when the father of the family
spent an hour in the evening teaching
Susan and her brothers to write; or when
the careful mother took him in hand to
help her in balancing her accounts, and
ascertaining that she owed no one a
penny, before she ventured upon any new
purchase. Then my worthy friend was
in his glory; and it was delightful to see
how he enjoyed his work. He had but
one fault, which was a tendency to splut-
ter; and as he was obliged to keep that
under restraint while engaged in writing,
he made himself amends by a little praise
of himself, when relating his exploits to a
sympathizing friend like myself. On his
return with the inkstand to the corner of
my shelf, he could not resist sometimes
boasting when he had not made a single
blot; or confessing to me, in perfect con-
fidence, how much the thinness of Susan's
up-strokes, or the thickness of her down-

strokes, was owing to the clearness of his slit or the fineness of his nib.

The family of which we made part lived frugally and worked hard, but they were healthy and happy. The father with his boys went out early in the morning to the daily labor by which they maintained the family. The mother remained at home, to take care of the baby and do the work of the house. She was the neatest and most careful person I ever saw, and she brought up her daughter Susan to be as notable as herself.

Susan was an industrious little girl, and in her childish way worked almost as hard as her mother. She helped to sweep the house, and nurse the baby, and mend the clothes, and was as busy as a bee. But she was always tidy; and though her clothes were often old and shabby, I never saw them dirty or ragged. Indeed, I must own that, in point of *neatness*, Susan was even superior to my old friend Rose. Rose would break her strings, or lose her buttons, or leave holes in her gloves, till reproved by her Mamma for untidiness; but Susan never forgot that "a stitch in

time saves nine," and the stitch was never
wanting. She used to go to school for
some hours every day: and I should have
liked to go with her, and help her in her
studies, especially when I found that she
was learning the multiplication-table, and
I remembered how useful I had been to
Rose in that very lesson; but dolls were
not allowed at school, and I was obliged
to wait patiently for Susan's company till
she had finished all her business, both at
school and at home.

She had so little time to bestow upon
me, that at first I began to fear that I
should be of no use to her. The sus-
picion was terrible; for the wish to be
useful has been the great idea of my life.
It was my earliest hope, and it will be my
latest pleasure. I could be happy under
almost any change of circumstances; but
as long as a splinter of me remained, I
should never be able to reconcile myself
to the degradation of thinking that I had
been *of no use*.

But I soon found I was in no danger of
what I so much dreaded. In fact, I
seemed to be even more useful to Susan

than to Rose. Before I had been long in
the house, she said one evening that she
had an hour to spare, and that she would
make me some clothes.

"Well and good," answered her mother;
"only be sure to put your best work in
them. If you mind your work, the doll
will be of great use to you, and you can
play without wasting your time."

This was good hearing for Susan and
me, and she spent most of her leisure in
working for me. While she was thus employed, I came down from my shelf, and
was treated with as much consideration
as when Rose and her companions waited
at my table.

A great change took place in my wardrobe. Rose had always dressed me in gay
silks and satins, without much regard to
underclothing; for, she said, as my gowns
must be sewn on, what did any petticoats
signify? So she sewed me up, and I
looked very smart; and if there happened to be any unseemly cobbling, she
hid it with beads or spangles. Once I
remember a very long stitch baffled all
her contrivances, and she said I must

pretend it was a new-fashioned sort of embroidery.

But Susan scorned all *makeshifts.* Nothing could have been more unfounded than my fears of becoming ragged or dirty. My attire was plain and suited to my station, but most scrupulously finished. She saw no reason why my clothes should not be made to take off and on, as well as if I had been a doll three feet high. So I had my plain gingham gowns with strings and buttons; and my shifts and petticoats run and felled, gathered and whipped, hemmed and stitched, like any lady's; and everything was neatly marked with my initial S. But what Susan and I were most particularly proud of was a pair of stays. They were a long time in hand, for the fitting them was a most difficult job; but when finished they were such curiosities of needlework, that Susan's neat mother herself used to show off the stitching and the eyelet-holes to every friend that came to see her.

Among them, Sarah the housemaid, who was sister to Susan's father, often called in to ask after us all. She was left

in charge of the house where my former
friends had lived, and they sometimes
sent her commissions to execute for them.
Then she was sure to come and bring us
news of *the family*, as she always called
Rose and her relations. Sometimes she
told us that Master William was a little
better; sometimes that she heard Miss
Rose was very much grown; she had generally something to tell that we were all
glad to hear. One evening, soon after
my apparel was quite completed, I was
sitting on my trunk as pleased with myself as Susan was with me, when Sarah's
head peeped in at the door.

"Good-evening to you all," said she; "I
thought as I went by you would like to
hear that I have a letter from the family,
and all's well. I have got a pretty little
job to do for Master Willy. He is to
have a set of new shirts sent out directly,
made of very fine, thin calico, because his
own are too thick. See, here is the stuff
I have been buying for them."

"It is beautiful calico, to be sure," said
Susan's mother; "but such fine stuff as
that will want very neat work. I am

afraid you will hardly be able to make
them yourself."

"Why, no," answered Sarah, smiling
and shaking her head. "I am sorry to
say, *there* comes in my old trouble, not
having learned to work neatly when I was
young. Take warning by me, Susan, and
mind your needlework nowadays. If I
could work as neatly as your mother, my
mistress would have made me lady's maid
and housekeeper by this time. But I
could not learn any but rough work,
more's the pity: so I say again, take
warning by *me*, little niece; take pattern
by your mother."

Susan looked at me and smiled as much
as to say, "I have taken pattern by her;"
but she had not time to answer, for Sarah
continued, addressing the mother: "How
I wish you could have time to do this
job, for it would bring you in a pretty
penny, and I know my mistress would
be pleased with your work; but they are
to be done very quickly, in time for the
next ship, and I do not see that you *could*
get through them with only one pair of
hands."

"We have two pair of hands," cried Susan, "here are mine."

"Ah, but what can they do?" asked Sarah, "and how can they do it? It is not enough to have four fingers and a thumb. Hands must be handy."

"And so they are," answered Susan's mother. "See whether any hands could do neater work than that." And she pointed me out to Sarah.

Sarah took me up, and turned me from side to side. Then she looked at my hems, then at my seams, then at my gathers, while I felt truly proud and happy, conscious that not a long stitch could be found in either.

"Well, to be sure!" exclaimed she, after examining me all over; "do you mean that all that is really Susan's own work?"

"Every stitch of it," replied the mother; "and I think better need not be put into any shirt, though Master William does deserve the best of everything."

"You never said a truer word, neither for Master William nor for little Susan," replied Sarah; "and I wish you joy, Susan,

of being able to help your mother so
nicely, for now I can leave you the job
to do between you."

She then told them what was to be the
payment for the work, which was a matter I did not myself understand, though I
could see that it gave them great satisfaction.

The money came at a most convenient
time, to help in fitting out Susan's brother
Robert for a place which had been offered
to him in the country. It was an excellent place; but there were several things,
as his mother well knew, that poor Robert
wanted at starting, but would not mention
for fear his parents should distress themselves to obtain them for him. Both
father and mother had been saving for
the purpose, without saying anything
about it to Robert; but they almost de-
spaired of obtaining more than half the
things they wanted, till this little sum of
money came into their hands so oppor-
tunely.

The father was in the secret, but Robert could scarcely believe his eyes, when
one evening his mother and Susan laid on

the table before him, one by one, all the useful articles he wished to possess. At first he seemed almost more vexed than pleased, for he thought of the saving and the slaving that his mother must have gone through to gain them; but when she told him how much of them was due to his little sister's neatness and industry, and how easy the work had been when shared between them, he was as much pleased as Susan herself.

We were all very happy that evening, including even the humble friends on the shelf; for I sat on my trunk, and related to the Pen how useful I had been in teaching Susan to work; and the worthy pen stood bolt upright in his inkstand, and confided to me with honest pride, that Robert had been chosen to his situation on account of his excellent writing.

Time passed on, and I suppose we all grew older, as I noticed from time to time various changes that seemed to proceed from that cause. The baby, for instance, though still going by the name of " Baby," had become a strong, able-bodied child, running alone, and very difficult to keep out of mischief. The most effectual way of keeping her quiet was to place me in her hands, when she would sit on the floor nursing me by the hour together, while her mother and sister were at work.

Susan was become a tall, strong girl, more notable than ever, and, like Rose before her, she gradually bestowed less attention on me; so that I was beginning to feel myself neglected, till on a certain birthday of her little sister's, she declared her intention of making me over altogether to the baby-sister for a birthday present. Then I once more rose into importance, and found powers which I thought declining, still undiminished. The baby gave a scream of delight when I was placed in her hand as her own. Till then she had only possessed one toy in the world, an old wooden horse, in comparison with which I seemed in the full bloom of youth and beauty. This horse, which she called Jack, had lost not merely the ornaments of mane and tail, but his head, one fore and one hind leg; so that nothing remained of the once noble quadruped but a barrel with the paint scratched off, rather insecurely perched upon a stand with wheels. But he was a faithful animal, and did his work to the last. The baby used to tie me on to his barrel, and Jack and I were drawn round and round the kitchen with as much satisfaction to our mistress, as in the days when I shone forth in my gilt coach with its four prancing piebalds.

But the baby's treatment of me, though gratifying from its cordiality, had a roughness and want of ceremony that affected my enfeebled frame. I could not conceal from myself that the infirmities I had observed in other dolls were gradually gaining ground upon me. Nobody ever said a harsh word to me, or dropped a hint of my being less pretty than ever, and the baby called me "Beauty, beauty," twenty times a day, but still I knew very well that not only had my rosy color and fine hair disappeared, but I had lost the whole of one leg and half of the other, and the lower joints of both my arms. In fact, as my worthy friend the Pen observed, both he and I were reduced to stumps.

The progress of decay caused me no

regret, for I felt that I had done my work,
and might now gracefully retire from
public life, and resign my place to newer
dolls. But though contented with my lot,
I had still one anxious wish ungratified.
The thought occupied my mind in-
cessantly; and the more I dwelt upon it,
the stronger grew the hope that I might
have a chance of seeing my old first friends
once more. This was now my only remaining care.

News came from them from time to
time. Sarah brought word that Master
William was better; that they had left
Madeira, and gone travelling about else-
where. Then that the father had been in
England upon business, and gone back
again; that Mr. Edward had been over to
foreign parts one summer holidays to see
his family, and on his return had come to
give her an account of them.

Sarah was always very bustling when
she had any news to bring of the family,
but one day she called on us in even more
flurry than usual. She was quite out of
breath from eagerness.

" Sit down and rest a minute before you

begin to speak," said her quiet sister-in-law. "There must be some great news abroad. It seems almost too much for you."

Sarah nodded, and began to unpack a great parcel she had brought with her.

"It don't seem bad news, to judge by your face," said the other; for now that Sarah had recovered breath, her smiles succeeded one another so fast, that she seemed to think words superfluous.

"I guess, I guess," cried Susan. "They are coming home."

"They are, indeed," answered Sarah at last; "they are coming home as fast as steam-engines can bring them: and here is work more than enough for you and mother till they come. Miss Margaret is going to be married, and you are to make the wedding clothes."

So saying, she finished unpacking her parcel, and produced various fine materials which required Susan's neatest work.

"These are for you to begin with," said she, "but there is more coming." She then read a letter from the ladies with directions about the needlework, to which

Susan and her mother listened with great attention. Then Sarah jumped up, saying she must not let the grass grow under her feet, for she had plenty to do. The whole house was to be got ready; and she would not have a thing out of its place, nor a speck of dust to be found, for any money.

Susan and her mother lost no time either; their needles never seemed to stop: and I sat on the baby's lap watching them, and enjoying the happy anticipation that my last wish would soon be accomplished.

But though Susan was as industrious as a girl could be, and just now wished to work harder than ever, she was not doomed to "all work and no play;" for her father took care that his children should enjoy themselves at proper times. In summer evenings, after he came home from his work, they used often to go out all together for a walk in the nearest park, when he and his wife would rest under the trees, and read over Robert's last letter, while the children amused themselves. Very much we all enjoyed it, for even I was seldom left behind. Susan would please the baby by dressing me in my best clothes for the walk, and the good-natured father would laugh merrily at us, and remark how much good the fresh air did me. We were all very happy; and when my thoughts travelled to other scenes and times, I sometimes wondered whether my former friends enjoyed themselves as much in their southern gardens as this honest family in their English fields.

Our needlework was finished and sent to Sarah's care to await Margaret's arrival, for which we were very anxious.

On returning home one evening after our walk, we passed, as we often did, through the street in which I had formerly lived. Susan was leading her little sister, who, on her part, clutched me in a way very unlike the gentleness which Susan bestowed upon her. On arriving at the well-known house, we saw Sarah standing at the area-gate. We stopped to speak to her.

"When are they expected?" asked Susan's mother.

"They may be here any minute," answered Sarah: "Mr. Edward has just brought the news."

The street-door now opened, and two gentlemen came out and stood on the steps. One was a tall, fine-looking boy, grown almost into a young man; but I could not mistake the open, good-humored countenance of my old friend Edward. The other was older, and I recognized him as the traveller who used to describe Madeira to Willy.

They did not notice us, for we stood back so as not to intrude, and their minds were evidently fully occupied with the expected meeting. We all gazed intently down the street, every voice hushed in eager interest. Even my own little mistress, usually the noisiest of her tribe, was silent as myself. It was a quiet street and a quiet time, and the roll of the distant carriages would scarcely have seemed to break the silence, had it not been for our intense watching, and hoping that the sound of every wheel would draw nearer. We waited long, and were more than once disappointed by carriages passing us and disappearing at the end of the street.

Edward and his friend walked up and down, east and west, north and south, in hopes of descrying the travellers in the remotest distance. But after each unavailing walk they took up their post again on the steps.

At last a travelling carriage laden with luggage turned the nearest corner, rolled toward us, and stopped at the house. The two gentlemen rushed down the steps, flung open the carriage-door, and for some moments all was hurry and agitation, and I could distinguish nothing. I much feared that I should now be obliged to go home without actually seeing my friends, for they had passed so quickly from the carriage to the house, and there had been so much confusion and excitement during those few seconds, that my transient glance scarcely allowed me to know one from another; but in course of time Sarah came out again, and asked Susan's father to help in unloading the carriage, desiring us to sit meanwhile in the housekeeper's room. So we waited till the business was finished, when, to my great joy, we were summoned to the sit-

ting-room, and I had the happiness of seeing all the family once more assembled.

I was delighted to find how much less
they were altered than I. I had been
half afraid that I might see one without a
leg, another without an arm, according to
the dilapidations which had taken place in
my own frame; but, strange to say, their
sensitive bodies, which felt every change
of weather, shrank from a rough touch,
and bled at the scratch of a pin, had out-
lasted mine, though insensible to pain or
sickness. There stood the father, scarcely altered; his hair perhaps a little more
gray, but his eyes as quick and bright as
ever. And there was the mother, still
grave and gentle, but looking less sad
and careworn than in the days of Willy's
constant illness. And there was, first in
interest to me, my dear mistress, Rose, as
tall as Margaret, and as handsome as Edward. I could not imagine her conde-
scending to play with me now. Margaret
looked just as in former times, good and
graceful, but she stood a little apart with
the traveller friend by her side, and I
heard Rose whisper to Susan that the

wedding was to take place in a fortnight.
They were only waiting for Geoffrey to
arrive. His ship was daily expected, and
they all wished him to be present.

And Willy, for whose sake the long
journey had been made, how was he?
Were all their hopes realized? Edward
shook his head when Susan's mother asked
that question, but Willy was there to answer it himself. He was standing by the
window, leaning on a stick, it is true, but
yet able to stand. As he walked across
the room, I saw that he limped slightly,
but could move about where he pleased.
He still looked thin and pale, but the
former expression of suffering and distress
had disappeared, and his countenance was
as cheerful as his manner. I could see
that he was very much better, though
not in robust health like Edward. He
thanked Susan's mother for her kind in-
quiries, and said that, though he had not
become all that his sanguine brother
hoped, he had gained health more than
enough to satisfy himself; that he was
most thankful for his present condition and
independence; and that if he was not quite

so strong as other people, he hoped he
should at any rate make a good use of the
strength that was allowed him. Turning
to Edward, who still looked disappointed,
he continued: "Who could have ventured
to hope, Edward, three years ago, that
you and I should now be going to col-
lege together?" And then even Edward
smiled and seemed content.

As we turned to leave the room, Susan
and her little sister lingered for a moment
behind the others, and the child held me
up toward Rose. Rose started, and exclaimed, "Is it possible? It really *is* my
poor old Seraphina. Who would have
thought of her being still in existence?
What a good, useful doll she has been! I
really must give her a kiss once more for
old friendship's sake."

So saying, she kissed both me and the
baby, and we left the house.

And now there remains but little more
for me to relate. My history and my existence are fast drawing to an end; my
last wish has been gratified by my meeting with Rose, and my first hope realized
by her praise of my usefulness.

She has since given the baby a new doll, and I am finally laid on the shelf, to enjoy, in company with my respected friend the Pen, a tranquil old age. When he, like myself, was released from active work, and replaced by one of Mordan's patent steel, he kindly offered to employ his remaining leisure in writing from my dictation, and it is in compliance with his advice that I have thus ventured to record my experience.

That experience has served to teach me that, as all inanimate things have some destined use, so all rational creatures have some appointed duties, and are happy and well employed while fulfilling them.

With this reflection, I bid a grateful farewell to those young patrons of my race who have kindly taken an interest in my memoirs, contentedly awaiting the time when the small remnant of my frame shall be reduced to dust, and my quiet existence sink into a still more profound repose.

THE END.

CPSIA information can be obtained at www.ICGtesting.com
Printed in the USA
BVOW02s0317010616

450223BV00013B/153/P